TONY BRAZAS
No foot Prints on the CARPET

My 43 Years
Hollywood

To order additional copies of this book, contact:
Xlibris
1-888-795-4274
www.Xlibris.com
Orders@Xlibris.com

He wears a mask and his face grows to fit it.

—George Orwell

We are what we pretend to be so we must be careful about what we pretend to be.

—Kurt Vonnegut

Acknowledgement:

(1) Confess that I have intentionally omitted the people and the films that were not particularly fun to work on.

(2)Jeff Bridges

Eliot Cates

Kim Ruha

During my 43 years in Hollywood i wish to thank the following:

Elliot Cates

All the transportation members of local 399

The actors and crew from the following movies and television shows i've worked on.

Mccloud, the rockford files, starsky and hutch, matlock, diagnosis murder

Highway to heaven, little house on the prarie, washington behind closed

Doors, roots, elvis, w.c.and me, all the papazian hirsch projects,

The fabulous baker boys, models inc. Phenomenon,michael, she's so lovely

Face off, the generals daughter, what women want, seabiscuit, k pax

Iron man, the amateurs, a dog year, the open road, tron legacy

The mentalist, superstore, homecoming and all the projects that i have

Forgotten.

Nbc, cbs, abc-disney, amazon

1

A few years ago, when I considered writing about my career in the film industry, the last sentence of James Joyce's autobiographical work **A Portrait of the Artist as a Young Man** kept running through my mind. At the end of his boyhood saga he states, "I go to encounter...the reality of experience and forge in the smithy of my soul the uncreated conscience of my race."

Strange how the power of those words have stayed with me all these years. Many thanks to my class entitled Introduction to English Literature, when I was a student at Notre Dame Prep School in Sherman Oaks, C alifornia.

Although my life as a driver for countless celebrities throughout the past four decades has not been as profound as "forging the conscience of my race," my story is the reality of experience forged by my encounters with movie stars, producers, and directors, who in many ways reflected the varying conscience of their generation.

Very briefly I can summarize my childhood in Custer, Michigan as the typical "flicks and flecks" of growing up in a small town. To this day when I think of Michigan I think "mosquitoes." When I think of California I think "no mosquitoes." I guess that says it all with one exception. I have remained a loyal Tigers, Pistons, and Lions fan my whole life. In 1965 my parents, Tony and Antoinette (Toni) Brazas, moved to Sherman Oaks, California to be close to my sister Delores (21 years my senior) who was in Hollywood, seeking a career as an actress. My brother Joe, who was ten years older than I, was serving in the United States Army so it was just my parents and me, residing at 4901 Tyrone Street. My father opened a restaurant named Toni's after my mother on Ventura Boulevard and Sunnyslope, where he served sandwiches, fried chicken and short ribs. The structure is still there today, but now it is a sushi restaurant known as Bizen.

I was thirteen years old when we moved and as I mentioned earlier I attended Notre Dame Prep School. My real education, however, began with a crush on Doris Day, who frequented our restaurant. She loved my dad's fried chicken and came in at least once a week for carry out. She always made a point of saying "hi" to me when I was helping my dad out. More importantly, I met

Dick Gautier, who played Heimi on the television show **Get Smart.** When I expressed an interest in television and film, Dick invited me to visit the Goldwyn Studios off Formosa Avenue and that's when everything really began.

Many days I would take the bus with my studio pass in hand, enter the main gate of Goldwyn Studios as if I was an important film star and watch the filming of **Get Smart** and **Hogan's Heroes.** I enjoyed watching Bob Crane and John Banner rehearse their scenes the most. They very often had to do take after take because they would crack-up the entire crew along with themselves in scene after scene. No one seemed to care, even the director, because the end product of all their screwing around was so good once they managed to get a final take. On other days I viewed the filming of **Gomer Pyle.** In my youthful naïveté I was excited when Jim Nabors took an interest in me by encouraging me to sit on his lap. One day I even got the opportunity to rehearse lines with Larry Storch, famous later for **F Troop,** who was a guest star on the show.

My sister Delores' house on Oakfield Drive in Sherman Oaks was four doors from the soon-to-be-famous Clint Eastwood. Clint's wife Maggie and my sister became friends and I enjoyed the Eastwood's company when they were dinner guests at our house many times. What I remember most about Clint was how quiet and unpretentious he was, but as a typical teenager I didn't hang around very much when the adults started talking about all kinds of things I wasn't interested in.

Of all my boyhood encounters in Hollywood, the one that stands out the most is meeting Moe Howard of Three Stooges fame. Once again Delores was instrumental in the event. Delores' mother-in-law, Lydia, played bridge with Moe's wife. When Delores told her how thrilled I would be to meet one of the Three Stooges, she had Moe's wife invite me to have lunch with Moe.

You can imagine my surprise and awe when Delores and I rang the doorbell at Moe's Bel-Air estate and Moe actually answered the door. He was having trouble breaking as a result of emphysema, but I will never forget his first words to me. He said, "Hello, pudding head." I started laughing and with my sister's introduction he extended his hand and as we shook hands I simply and nervously said, "Nice to meet you, Moe."

I wish I could remember more about the hour I spent with him. As I reflect, I can't remember what was served for lunch or our conversation with the exception of one of my biggest faux pas of all time. I was talking about one of my favorite Three Stooges episodes entitled "Three Little Pigskins" co-starring a very young Lucille Ball, where the stooges are mistaken for three football stars. In my excitement I actually told Moe that Curly was my favorite. Gentleman that he was, he took my remark in his stride and said, "I think he was everyone's favorite." Later in my career, this lunch with Moe Howard would play an important role in cementing my friendship with Mel Gibson, a huge Three Stooges fan.

After these brushes with a few celebrities, my time was spent over the next few years finishing my education at Notre Dame, followed by two years at Valley Junior College. Through a girlfriend at VJC, I got a job at Universal Studios, where I supplied the souvenir shops and occasionally worked at the Universal Gift Shop counter. While at Universal, I saw up close and personal such luminaries as Alfred Hitchcock, Edith Head (famous fashion designer for the movies), James Stewart, Valerie Perrine, James Garner and Robert Blake. At the time, I never dreamed that I would be working with them some day.

Within a year I broke with Universal to attend UCLA, but realized very early that the academic life was not for me. I wanted to make some money. It was 1975 and I finally bit the bullet and joined the Teamsters Union-The Studio Division of Drivers. I didn't know it at the time, but that was the best decision of my life.

As a new member of the Teamsters Union at Universal Transportation, I was assigned to a feature film entitled **W. C. and Me** starring Rod Steiger as W. C. Fields in this autobiographical homage to the great comedian. Valerie Perrine was his co-star and she was very nice to everyone on the set. Little did I know that I would work with her almost thirty years later in **The Amateurs**. But that's the way it is in Hollywood, you run into cast and crew members from one production to another. I only encountered Rod Steiger a few times as I spent most of my time transporting background actors and running errands...a typical assignment for a new driver. My one memory of Steiger was his staying in career throughout the shoot, whenever I was close to the sets or locations.

During the first month of employment I worked on all kinds of driving related jobs where I met Dennis Weaver, who was filming his television series **McCloud** and James Garner, who was busy on his very popular series **The Rockford Files.** Garner ended up going on a few dates with my sister, who was a very pretty working actress cast in a number of guest star roles. What struck me about both Weaver and Garner was that their personalities on and off the screen were essentially the same.

The Universal Amphitheater was, of course, located on the Universal Lot. After a day's work, another driver and I always enjoyed listening to the many concerts performed there. One evening we were assigned to take some speakers to the theater because John Denver had requested them for his concert on that particular night. To my good fortune, when we unloaded the speakers, John was standing near the stage next to his manager. He came over to me and said, "Hello," making sure we had brought the proper speakers. I was a huge fan so when he struck up a conversation with me I was delighted. He was one of the easiest guys to talk with that I have ever met. He had the kind of personality that made you feel like we had known each other for a long time. I told him that I was reading the motivational book **E. S. T.** by Werner Erhard. E. S. T. (Erhard Seminar Training) was a self-awareness/self-help book designed to make you think positively about yourself and to see yourself winning your dream. Remember it was the mid-70's. John told me that putting my energy into improving myself and winning my dream was the best thing someone my age could do. He smiled that famous grin and said, "Always think big, Tony."

Within the next few months I moved to Paramount Studios and I was still attending the E. S. T. classes on weekends. **Looking for Mr. Goodbar** was being filmed there and I drove Diane Keaton for a few weeks. A rare opportunity for someone so new to the union. Like Valerie Perrine, Diane was very nice to me and everyone on the set. I think she was struggling with her role in the film. Although she really didn't talk to me about it, my impression was that she was very young (only a few years older than I), shy and quiet and her role was a gigantic stretch for her. But as everyone knows she was go good in it she became an instant star.

Following **Looking for Mr. Goodbar**, I drove for the television mini-series **Washington Behind Closed Doors** written by the famous/infamous John Erlichman. The script centered around what Erlichman called "the Richard Nixon power trip." During the filming I hung out with Jason Robards and Cliff Robertson, who always took their work very seriously, but never seemed to have to stay in character throughout the day. We had fun talking about sports and girls mostly. Andy Griffith was also in the cast and he always had his guitar, often serenading us between scenes. He loved the country ballads and encouraged people to sing along as he sang and picked away. Unfortunately, a lot of the cast and crew couldn't sing very well, but it never bothered Andy.

My E. S. T. classes on the weekends were going well and I foresaw much success in the movie business. One of the most important assignments my instructor gave me was to postulate in written form where I saw myself in relation to achieving my life' goal. I postulated: I will be a success in whatever I pursue in the motion picture and television business. After I had written it on a piece of paper, I folded it and stuck it in the wall of Paramount's Soundstage Number 30. It is probably still there.

The Monday after I completed my E. S. T. classes and stuck that postulated goal in the soundstage wall, I was assigned to the feature **Marathon Man** as Laurence Olivier's driver. I would pick him and his butler up in Beverly Hills and drive him to location at the Arboretum in Arcadia. Those morning drives were always a pleasure. He would reminisce about his affairs with Joan Fontaine and Veronica Lake as well as many other starlets whose names escape me. Strangely, he never mentioned his wife Vivian Leigh and I was afraid to ask him anything about her. He was a wonderful, jovial man and a smile always comes to my face when I think of him. His butler said very little and I learned early on that Mr. Olivier liked to do most of the talking...especially about himself. Although he liked to catalogue his many affairs, he strictly adhered to the Gentleman's Code and, unfortunately, gave no serious details.

Following **Marathon Man** I worked on another Paramount television series called **Busting Loose** starring Adam Arkin. The series was shot almost solely on the lot and during the course of shooting Adam and I became friends. **Busting Loose** was shot on Friday nights before a studio audience. Prior to the evening shoot Adam and I would always play basketball with the guys filming **Happy Days**, who also shot before a studio audience. There was always Adam and me and usually Ron

Howard, Donny Most and Anson Williams plus some guys from each crew. Henry Winkler never played, but for the rest of us it was like we were all back in high school again. The guys from **Happy Days** were damn good and they usually won.

After Friday night's filming, Bob Elsey (another Teamster) and I would have to board an old station wagon and take the film to the camera department, which was across the lot, for development. I sat 'shotgun' and Bob drove the station wagon. While he held a beer in one hand and the rest of the six pack between his legs, he would speed through "the tank" (a sunken area at Paramount that could be filled with water for all kinds of nautical scenes) and end up at the camera department. Crazy as Bob was, there were never any accidents or problems. The film always arrived on time and in one piece.

One of my favorite tasks was delivering scripts. Since there was no internet in those days I had to deliver the scripts by hand. Paramount would give me a stack of scripts to be delivered to actors, directors, and producers. It was always fun because I had the opportunity to visit the homes of many famous people, most of whom are gone now. As a twenty-one year old kid just starting out, I had all these illusions about the kinds of houses the movie stars lived in and for the most part I was never disappointed. I remember most the Beverly Hills deliveries with the imperial palms standing like sentries along the immaculately cut lawns and stately homes. I would, for instance, cross Lexington and Roxbury Drive where James Stewart lived on one corner and Lucille Ball on the other corner. I would make deliveries there and then drive to Richard Widmark's house on the opposite corner. Up the street I delivered scripts to Gregory Peck and Robert Mitchum, who was either stoned or intoxicated when I handed him his script.

Barry Diller was the CEO for Paramount Pictures and Television in those days and I would have to deliver scripts to his home. Impressed with my demeanor and work ethic, he took me under his wing and made me a liaison between the studio and him. He let me drive his 12-cylinder Jaguar XKE from his house to the studio and very often I would drive around Los Angeles, playing the part of a movie mogul. I wonder to this day if he ever checked the mileage. As I reflect even if he would have checked the miles, he was the kind of guy who wouldn't have cared.

My last assignment at Paramount was to drive Mae West home from the studio every night after shooting **Sextet**, her last picture. I drove her to the Ravenswood Apartments on Rossmore, where she lived until she died from a stroke soon after filming. In her whole career she only made thirteen movies, but to movie buffs around the world she is remembered as one of the greatest sex symbols along with Jean Harlowe and Marilyn Monroe. To most people's surprise, she made a fortune investing in real estate throughout Los Angeles and the San Fernando Valley. Like Fred MacMurray, Bob Hope and Randloph Scott, Mae had the good sense to invest in land.

Just like the characters she played on the screen, Mae had a risqué sense of humor and she loved to tease. Even at her age she was a bit of a "cock-tease." The last night I drove her home as I pulled in front of her apartment, she said to me, "You know, Tony, you're a good looking boy. You could have been a movie star. If I were a little younger you could come up and see me tonight." She laughed and when I walked her to the door she gave me a little kiss on the cheek and said, "Thanks."

I opened the door and she walked in. I never saw her again, but to this day I wonder if I could have made love to one of the greatest sex symbols of movie history that night.

3

After my stay at Paramount Studios I worked as a dispatcher at CBS - Radford right off Ventura Boulevard in Studio City, which is CBS's main lot. Many old time westerns were made on this lot when it was Republic Studios. After CBS bought it the network continued to grind out weekly westerns like **Gunsmoke** and **The Rifleman** there.

Having worked almost non-stop for the past few years, I decided it was time for a vacation. A good friend, Jim Boysen, and I decided to take a couple months off and go to Europe. I guess we both thought we had been over-worked and needed a little R and R from the industry. When I returned from Europe, I went to Warner Bros., where I resumed my role as a driver.

At Warner's I was assigned to drive during the production of the monumental television mini-series **Roots** with LaMar Burton, Cecily Tyson, and Jay Simpson among many other stars. My most memorable encounter was with one of my favorite boyhood heroes Chuck Connors of **The Rifleman** fame. Chuck and I got along very well on the set and he eventually told me that he liked me so well because I reminded him of his sons, who worked in the grip department.

One morning a stunt man showed up, not recalling his name, showed up on the set at the same time as Chuck. For some strange reason, the stunt man, and Chuck staged a mock-fight in front of all the background players. They wrestled around a bit and when they stopped the background players, in confusion and awe, were still intently watching the stars. Chuck turned to them and in his best surly snarl said to them, "What are you staring at? Do you think I'm Jesus Christ?" The background players began averting their eyes, muttering to themselves as they walked away. I can only imagine what they were saying about Chuck. After his questions, I'm sure it was nothing good.

From the lengthy production of **Roots,** I next worked with Dick Clark on his made for television production of **Elvis**, starring Kurt Russell in the title role. Although Dick Clark had never had Elvis Presley on his iconic teenage dance show **American Bandstand**, he had been obsessed with the King of Rock-n-Roll his entire life. This film was the first of two he made for television, both of which revolved around Elvis' "rags to riches" story that is so much a part of American rock history. During this picture I interacted with Dick, but our paths did not really cross very often and I didn't get to know him. That would come later when I coincidentally worked on his second Elvis picture. On the other hand, Kurt Russell and I, who were about the same age, enjoyed talking with each other. We found that we shared the same interests, and all the other stuff guys talk about. Kurt spoke very fondly of his father Bing, a character actor who appeared in countless westerns, and played the sheriff in twelve seasons in Bonanza. He gave me the impression that Bing was truly a hero in his eyes and I know he wished that his father could have had the success that he was blessed with.

One day I was assigned to drive for the construction crew, who had to create the gates at the entrance to Graceland. On that day I did very little driving. Instead, I helped the crew cut out the plywood notes and figures that appeared on the gates. Much later, when the location shooting wrapped, we had a couple of weeks of cleaning up to do. Ronnie Kraft, the painter, had a sister was totally in love with Elvis. I think her name was Pam and Ronnie kept saying, "Pam would love to have these gates." To no one's surprise the last day of clean up the Graceland gates disappeared. We found out later that Ronnie had transported them to Pam's house in Hemet.

The story of the Graceland gates became more interesting fourteen years later when I coordinated the transportation for Dick's other Elvis picture entitled **Elvis and the Colonel: The Untold Story**. Beau Bridges played the Colonel and Rob Youngblood played Elvis. I was the only member of the crew who knew Dick so on the first day he introduced himself and me to the cast and crew. After the introduction, the two of us went into his office for a production meeting. He told me the scheduling of the picture for the first week, which was primarily exterior shots. Then he began complaining that he couldn't find the Graceland gates, which he had used in the earlier picture **Elvis.** He said, "I really want to use those gates. It will save me a lot of money if I don't have to re-make them. No one knows where they are or if they even still exist." I, of course, responded, "I think I know where the gates are located." He did a double take and I told him that they were probably still in Pam's possession to which he said, "You get on the phone immediately and talk to her. Your job is to get those gates back."

I was the only driver at the time, since shooting hadn't begun, so I procured a flatbed truck, got Pam's telephone number from Ronnie and called her. She told me that she still had the gates and I could pick them up for the production.

Arriving at her house in Hemet, I was shocked to see the Graceland gates, minus the notes and figures that we had made, leaning against her carport, exposed for many years to the southern California sun and nature in general. They were rusty and what remained of the paint was blistered and peeling. Pam had seen me drive up and had come outside to greet me as I examined the gates. After saying hello to one another, I asked her what had happened to the notes and figures. She said, "Oh, I still have them. I didn't want them to get damaged."

She led me into the house and while I waited she retrieved them, bringing them out in a clothes bag. They had been lying under her bed for the past fourteen years. Unlike the gate, they were in perfect condition. Thanking her for preserving the notes and figures, I loaded the gates in the flatbed and placed the clothes bag on the seat next to me. Just outside of Hemet I called Dick's office to let him know that I had accomplished my mission. When I arrived at the studio, I gave everything to the construction crew and within a couple of days the gates looked just as if they were the real thing.

After that mission I could do no wrong in the eyes of Dick Clark, who was very much like Michael Landon...a man who enjoyed his work and treated everyone on the set with equal respect. He was a true gentleman. Two decades later I saw Dick when I was working on **The Mentalist.** We were filming at his beach property in Malibu, which he called Gulls Way, right off the Pacific Coast Highway. He was still recovering from a stroke earlier in the year and everyday he would come out of the house to go to therapy. One day I re-introduced myself and he began laughing when he remembered me. The first thing out of his mouth was, "Remember those Graceland gates, Tony?"

I said, "Yeah. I had to drive all the way to Hemet for them."

He responded with, "I always appreciated that. You saved me some money."

He told me that he had the Graceland gates displayed in Dick Clark's 57 Heaven Automobile Museum in Branson, Missouri. In 2009 Mecum Auction sold the entire contents of the museum when it went out of business. The infamous Graceland gates could very well be in the hands of another Elvis fan today.

Returning to the late 70's where I was still working at CBS - Radford, I was assigned to **The Magic of Lassie**, which starred not only Lassie but also James Stewart. Prior to shooting I worked at the production office with Jack Wrather and Bonita Granville. Bonita had been an old time actress and she along with Jack owned the rights to the **Lassie** pictures and **The Lone Ranger**. When filming began they assigned me to drive Lassie (there were actually five Lassies), Rudd Weatherwax, the owner of Lassie, and his brother Robert. I should also mention that all five Lassies were male dogs, whose disposition was considered better for film work than the female collies.

My job was to drive Rudd, Robert and the 'Lassie of the Day" back to Malibu, where the kennel was located. Rudd, who was still in mourning after the recent death of his wife, was drinking heavily. Everyday after shooting we would leave CBS-Radford and wind through the Laurel Canyon neighborhoods, turn right on Laurel Canyon and make a left on Moorpark, where Rudd's favorite liquor store was located. I always parked the van in the same location...a space next to a patch of grass between the curb and the sidewalk. One night, there was only one Lassie with us. When Rudd opened the door to leave the van and go into the liquor store Lassie jumped out. Rudd, who had already had a few drinks, started going berserk, "There goes my fuckin' money. Tony, go catch Lassie." For all Rudd's excitement, Lassie just wanted to take a leak. He peed on a nearby fire hydrant, momentarily sniffed around, sat down, staring at me. When I brought my hand to my thigh, he automatically came to Rudd who was standing next to me and jumped back in the van. A lot of drama on Rudd's part dissipated and he went into the liquor store for his evening "medication." I kept thinking that it would have been my ass if Lassie would have run onto Moorpark and been hit by a car. Can you imagine the headline the next day?

The real treat for me while working on the picture was driving James Stewart home many nights. He had always been one of my favorite actors and I had delivered scripts to his home in Beverly Hills, but never met him. As I mentioned earlier, he lived on Roxbury across from Lucille Ball. Every night I would park the car and walk him to the door, where his wife, Gloria, would greet us. He always insisted on giving me a five dollar tip. At first I refused, but after his coaxing in the famous Jimmy Stewart cadence…"Now … you … just… take …this money, young man." I couldn't resist and took the five dollars. He was the one and only person to ever tip me, which is never expected in the business.

My next project was **The Pursuit of D. B. Cooper**, a film that speculated on how D. B. Cooper planned and got away with over $100,000 in 1974, when he bailed out of a 727 airliner over a remote area south of Seattle, Washington with the cash. John Frankenheimer began directing the film in a very remote location with Treat Williams starring as Cooper. Shooting was on the Snake River in Idaho and we were accommodated in Jackson Hole, Wyoming. This meant we had a four hour round trip every day for the shoot.

During the first two weeks, Frankenheimer was totally out of control on this location shoot. In those days the Steady-Cam camera did not exist. Instead, for action shots in cars or boats, for instance, cameras were mounted on Tyler mounts attached to the vehicle. This type of shooting is most familiar to film fans as it was the technique used to film the car chase in Steve McQueen's **Bullit**. The premise of the film was that Cooper had escaped down a river on an inflatable raft after his jump from the 727 airliner. Frankenheimer wanted to re-create his escape in the most realistic format possible at the time, which incorporated cameras mounted on boats to film the raft. Within the first two weeks of shooting, Frankenheimer was responsible for losing two cameras, totaling $500,000, in the Snake River. Equally, he had employed a number of expensive helicopters with Tyler mounted cameras to capture the aerial shots he needed. Added to these expenses, he had a lavishly catered dinner/party for the cast and crew every night. At the end of the first two weeks he had spent over $2,000,000…one quarter of the entire amount budgeted for the film. Compounding these expenses, the first set of dailies were lost in transit to Los Angeles for development. By the beginning of the third week of shooting Frankenheimer was fired.

Replaced by Roger Spottiswoode, the shoot went very smoothly once I came up with the solution to insure that the dailies were delivered to Los Angeles without any further losses. The solution was simple. I would hand deliver the day's film in one of the helicopters over the mountain from the Snake River (a 20 minute flight) to Jackson Hole Airport. This saved two hours of driving everyday around the mountain, which allowed Spottiswoode to film until sunset. Once I delivered the film, a PA from Los Angeles would fly in and then hand carry the film back to L. A. That became the day's routine and there was never another incident of lost dailies.

After the location work on **The Pursuit of D. B. Cooper** I returned to Los Angeles to work on **Raging Bull**, where I met Martin Scorsese. He always walked around the set with a small bottle of Afrin. No one knew what was actually in it but it seemed to keep him going during the day and/

or night. Scorsese always insisted on a quiet set...as little noise as possible. When my friend Eliot Cates played a photographer in **The Aviator** years later, he told me that Scorsese still insists on the least amount of noise on location and on the set. Eliot said that it was particularly difficult to accommodate his wish as they were shooting in Korea Town the nights he worked, but everyone did his best.

While shooting **Raging Bull** I drove Robert De Niro to his girlfriend's house in Encino every day when we wrapped. At the time the cell phone was just beginning to be used by those who could afford one. The damn things were very awkward and almost the size of a shoe box, weighing about two pounds. There were a limited amount of cell towers then and the reception could be very spotty. Going over the Sepulveda Pass on the 405 to Encino, De Niro would try to call his girlfriend and he would lose reception. Volatile as he was at the time (probably still in character from filming), whenever he lost reception in the pass, he would slam the cell phone on the back of the front seat until it ultimately broke. Then he would quickly roll down the window of the station wagon and throw it on the freeway. Every time he did this he would say after rolling up the window, "Tony, remember to keep at least a half dozen of these fuckers in the car at all times." And I would dutifully reply, "Will do, Mr. De Niro."

Completing **Raging Bull** a few of us got together and worked on the feature **The Man with Bogart's Face.** Robert Sacchi, the spitting image of Bogart, played the title role. The most fun on the shoot was meeting George Raft. When we wrapped on his scenes, I drove him to his condominium in Century City. He was so quiet and reflective I'm not sure we exchanged more than ten words.

Michelle Phillips of Mamas and Pappas fame also worked on the picture. Michelle and I hit it off right away. On the last day she worked I drove her home. When I opened the car door for her, she invited me into her West Los Angeles house. We drank some beer and fooled around on the couch. Here I'll take a page from Mr. Olivier and let you imagine what you like.

After **The Man with Bogart's Face** I worked for Chartoff-Winkler on a feature entitled **True Confessions** with Robert De Niro and Robert Duval. The film concerned the notorious Black Dahlia murders in Los Angeles in the 1930's. During the first few weeks of shooting, De Niro's engraved Oscar for **Raging Bull** had been finished and I was assigned to pick it up and deliver it to the Chateau Marmont where he was staying. After arriving at his residence, I reverently carried the Oscar to his room as if I were holding some sacred religious object. I knocked on the door gently and he answered while on the phone. Someone from the studio had called him so he knew I would be arriving with the statue.

He said, "How ya doin', Tony?"

And I said, "Just fine. I have a little something for you." I handed him the Oscar and he tossed it on the couch, where it bounced onto the carpeted floor.

He held his hand over the phone and said, "I'm gonna use it for a doorstop." Then added, "You want a drink?"

I said, "No, thank you. I can't. I'm working."

"Okay," he said. "Thanks for the delivery." I left and he resumed his telephone conversation.

With the exception of delivering the Oscar, much of my time was spent as the dispatcher on **True Confessions**, for which I basically ran the transportation department. One morning I got a call from Robert Chartoff's secretary. Chartoff, who was producing the film, wanted his lunch picked up from the Ivy in West Hollywood. She told me that he wanted the China at the office to be packed and brought to the restaurant where the waiters would place the meal on the China plate and I was to bring it back to the office. When I got her call we were extremely busy. We were close to running out of film on the set and all the transportation people were consumed by what seemed to me to be more important tasks than delivering a lunch to Mr. Chartoff. I apologized, saying "I'm sorry, but I don't have anyone that I can pull right now to come over without holding up production." The secretary replied, "Don't worry about getting the film to the set or anything else. He wants his lunch." I left the office and delivered the lunch myself. Taking care of his noon meal was the most important task and he was apparently willing to hold up production for its delivery. To this day I have no idea what the lunch consisted of, but I think Mr. Chartoff must have had a little Howard Hughes in him.

As 1981 approached I couldn't believe how fast my first few years had passed. With **True Confessions** in the can, the Chertoff-Winkler Production Company was in full swing and I began prepping for **Rocky III** to be shot at MGM Studios and on locations in Culver City.

The first time I met Sylvester Stallone was at a meeting where we were deciding what cars we would use for Stallone in the film. I explained to everyone that I had contacted Ferrari, thinking that their car with its iconic symbol would be the perfect choice for the Italian Stallion. Ferrari couldn't make a decision so time being of the essence I contacted Lamborghini. Unfortunately, Lamborghini expressed no interest at all. I added that Maserati, however, seemed somewhat enthused about providing cars for the production. The car choice was settled. It would be Maserati and within a few days the two cars we chose were on the lot. I couldn't believe it when, at the end of shooting, they gave Stallone both cars.

At the meeting Stallone wouldn't even talk to a "mere driver" like me. He always talked to me through our Line Producer. His superior attitude was completely crushed at the end of the meeting as all of us stood up. I'm six feet four inches tall and Stallone is, at the most, about five feet six inches tall. He wouldn't even stand next to me any time during the filming let alone talk to me or any of the other drivers, crew or background players.

I did become friends with Mr. T (Laurence Turraud). He and I had a standing racquetball game every Saturday at the Mid-Valley Racquet Club along with Jim Brubaker our UPM (Unit Production Manager). What was the most fun about playing racquetball with Mr. T was our mutual competitive nature. The game that stands out in my mind is when we were tied at one point. He gave me an incredibly difficult return and as I tried to reach the ball, I looked like a ballet dancer performing an aborted pirouette. Mr. T. couldn't stop laughing and with my youthful ego always in tack, I came on strong and won the match.

Throughout the **Rocky III** shoot, Stallone was very demanding. Although it is a cliché, prima donna always comes to mind when I think of him. A good example of this is a call I received on the first day of shooting. His assistant told me that Sly wants fresh lobster delivered everyday to his trailer for lunch. In the movie business everyone tries to accommodate the star of the picture, but in this case I decided to have a little fun. Sly did not specify that he wanted the lobster cooked...after all he said fresh lobster. I sent a driver to the Santa Monica Seafood Company, where he purchased two live lobsters for $100. Later that morning I mentioned Stallone's request to the Line Producer, who added up the cost for lobster everyday over a rather lengthy production and he hit the ceiling. He said, "No more lobster. Let him eat shrimp."

Knowing that the Line Producer had made the "shrimp decision." I knew this was my last chance to carry out my plan. While Stallone was in make-up, I took the lobsters to his trailer and placed the clanking crustations in the sink. When he entered his trailer after make-up, he was, of course, greeted by the clatter from the sink. Sly came running out of his trailer and yelled, "Whoever dropped those fuckin' lobsters in my sink is a real funny guy!" No one said a word as he angrily eyed everyone around the trailer, looking for the culprit, hoping for a response. He stormed back into his trailer and everyone started laughing. I know the Line Producer got his way. After that there were no more trips to the Santa Monica Seafood Company. I was glad I wasn't the director who had to work with him that day.

From 1980-1985 I drove for Blake Edwards off-and-on. The opposite of Stallone, Blake was a truly great guy to work for. The first movie I was assigned to was **10**. I drove Bo Derek from MGM Studios to Blake's house in Malibu after each day's shooting, where along with the director of photography and the editor, he and Bo would have dinner and watch the dailies. I was invited into the house every night and Julie Andrews, Blake's wife, always served us drinks. One night I talked with Julie, while she made fried chicken. I told her about Doris Day, who loved fried chicken, frequenting my father's restaurant when I was a teenager. She confessed that she had a love for fried chicken and that she had always been a Doris Day fan. While she fried the chicken I sipped a beer and we talked about all kinds of things. I told her about my sister, who was the same age as Julie, and how she had cut short her acting career to get married, which she never regretted. Julie was exactly like Blake...very down to earth and never acted as if she were above anyone else.

During one drive to Blake's house Bo confided in me that she really wanted to be a producer more than an actress. I kept thinking how beautiful she was and like everyone on the set we knew that **10** was going to be a success and that she would be a huge star. She was only twenty-one and I couldn't quite picture her as a producer, but I simply said, "Whatever you decide to do I know you'll be a big success." My old E.S.T. classes kicking in at the moment. She just laughed casually and said, "I hope you're right." By that time we were on PCH and she became very quiet. I know she was thinking about her future. Years later I was in Vancouver, working with Jeff Bridges on **Tron-Legacy**, and I ran into her. We agreed that working on **10** was one of our best filmmaking experiences because of the hospitality of Blake Edwards and Julie Andrews.

Thinking of Blake, I often recall working with stuntman Allen Graft on **Sunset.** In the film Blake directed Bruce Willis who was cast as silent movie star Tom Mix. To Bruce's credit he always liked to do as many of his own stunts as possible. One day Allen, one of the best stuntmen I've ever known, was working as an actor/stuntman opposite Bruce Willis in an important action sequence in what is purported to be a silent western movie being filmed. Allen played a cowboy who was to throw Bruce from the saloon into the street. Bruce had a bad shoulder at the time and Allen did not want to do anything that would cause more pain. As is the case in all pictures, the stuntman always coordinates the stunt with the actor. He asked Bruce if he wanted him to be as gentle as possible when he threw him through the saloon door.

Bruce said, "Hell no. Don't worry about my fuckin' shoulder. Just do it and make it look real."

Blake asked, "Are you sure, Bruce?"

Without another thought, Bruce said, "I want it to look real."

Blake in turn said, "Alright, then, let's do it."

When the camera rolled Allen took Bruce and threw him through the saloon doors as hard as he could. I swear Bruce landed at least fifteen feet in the street on his bad shoulder. Bruce was so sore after that scene, Blake had to wrap for the day, content that he had got exactly what he wanted. Both Bruce and Allen were relieved that they didn't have to do the shot again.

Outside his trailer I asked Bruce, "Why didn't you use a stuntman for the shot?"

Rubbing his shoulder, he said, "I'm not that kind of actor." Then he smiled and continued, "Go get me some Capzasin for this shoulder, Tony."

I said, "Sure thing" as he walked into his trailer still rubbing his shoulder.

I drove Dudley Moore on **Mickey and Maude** one of Blake's later pictures. Dudley struck me as a very lonely man after he and Susan Anton had parted. Very often he would invite me into his house, a beautiful place on the beach, located right at the end of South Marina del Rey by the Channel. We would have a glass of wine and he would play the piano for me as long as I had time to listen. He rarely had anything that he wanted to talk about. He just wanted an audience of at least one to listen to him play.

While working on Blake's film **Blind Date**, I had a momentous encounter with Kim Bassinger. One of my duties everyday was to make sure everything was proper in her trailer...it had been cleaned properly, the refrigerator was stocked with her choices, and all the appliances were in working order. To say the least, Kim was not a shy woman. One day before checking her trailer, I knocked on the door, which was protocol, just in case the star might have arrived early. To my surprise Kim answered the door with her robe open and didn't bother to close it. She was completely naked. I got a view of her that her fans could only dream of.

My next picture was Bob Fosse's **Star 80**, which went into production in June, 1982. This is the picture where Eric Roberts played Paul Snider, the husband of Dorothy Stratten, the famous Playboy Playmate. Mariel Hemingway played Dorothy whom he murdered in a jealous rage. I picked Eric up from his rented house above Fairfax in Hollywood and drove him to and from

Hollywood Center Studio or any given location site everyday for filming. Eric had some wacky ways of rehearsing. One day he was going to shoot a scene in a restaurant where he gets upset and argues with Mariel. As a method actor he prepared for the scene by smoking a bunch of cigarettes at 5:30 in the morning on our way to the location in Beverly Hills. On our drive, between each cigarette, he would stick his head out the town car window and scream like a chimpanzee in heat so his voice would be raspy for the scene.

One night Eric procured a couple of grams of this white powder and invited a group of actual Playboy Playmates to his house. They had been recruited that day to appear in the Playboy Mansion scene in the film. One thing led to another and before I knew it Eric and I were in his hot tube with three of the Playmates...clothing was optional.

Mariel and I became friends and even dated a little bit. Our relationship was nothing serious, but we had a lot of fun together. She lives in Westlake Village and I think sometimes that I'd like to see her over a cup of coffee after almost forty years.

When not driving Eric, I was assigned to drive Cliff Robertson who played Hugh Hefner. He lived at the Oakwood Gardens on Barham at the time. Like Eric, I picked him up and drove him home. He was an excellent tennis player and I was pretty good as well. We played tennis every night and he usually won. Cliff and I didn't talk too much, just played tennis, but I got the impression that he would rather be on the tennis court than the movie set.

Following **Star 80** I did a made for television movie starring Rock Hudson entitled **World War III**, directed by Boris Segal, the father of Katie Segal of **Married with Children** fame. On location Boris walked into the tail rotor of a helicopter as he was directing and was killed instantly. That was the only truly tragic experience I ever encountered on any movie location.

David Greene replaced him as director and I drove for him for a short time. Then I was assigned to pick up Rock Hudson at his home in Beverly Hills every morning. Every day I arrived, Rock's butler would serve me tea and toast, while I waited for Rock to finish his morning constitutional. Rock was a very generous and fun loving man and I still laugh when I remember him coming out of his bedroom every morning with his Asian boyfriend...they were all smiles.

5

Shot in Tucson and Old Tucson, Arizona my next picture was **Cannonball Run II**. That was quite an experience. I hung out with director Hal Needham and cast members Dean Martin, Burt Reynolds, Dom DeLuise, Sammy Davis, Jr. and Charles Nelson Reilly. One day Frank Sinatra, who was also in the picture, arrived and you would have thought that royalty had made a visit---in a way I guess it had. He had some business to discuss with Dean so the two of them talked in Dean's trailer and to our disappointment, Frank didn't interact with the rest of us. Sammy told me later that when Frank talked about business it was ALL BUSINESS, no fucking around.

Sammy and I became friends over the course of the picture. Once he felt comfortable working with me he would come out of his trailer every morning and literally jump into my arms. He was so small it was like holding a small child.

Watching Burt Reynolds and Dom DeLuise work together was always a riot. They reminded me of Bob Crane and John Banner when I watched them as a teenager on the set of **Hogan's Heroes**. Just when Needham, who was very patient, thought he had a usable take, Burt and Dom would start cracking up and the crew usually followed. There would be take after take until the two of them settled down and finally did the scene to comic perfection.

Hal would wrap everyday by 2 PM, which is extremely rare in the film and television business. All of us would go back to our Arizona Inn residence for a beautiful buffet with plenty of adult beverages. Every night was close to riotous and the stars would choose one of their peers to "roast." With Dom it was usually about his weight, Sammy his size, Dean his drinking and Burt his acting prowess. All of us would dine and drink together and the stars would continue to razz once another, while we watched the day's outtakes. In short, everyone would get totally hammered. To this day I have no idea when the actors learned their lines or, more importantly, how the picture actually got made.

I knew from our production meetings with Hal prior to leaving for Arizona, that everyone on the shoot loved to play practical jokes on one another. I was told that Burt Reynolds was only five feet eight inches tall and he was very self-conscious about his height. Another crew member and I were the first to arrive at the Arizona Inn the day before shooting because we had to deliver a tanning bed to Burt's room. We were in the Arizona sun at a beautiful time of year and for some reason he wanted to use a tanning bed. By this time in my career, however, there was really nothing that surprised me when it came to star's requests. Since we had to unpack the tanning bed, I decided to play a little joke on Burt. His clothes and cowboy boots had already arrived and had been placed in the closet. I removed all the lifts from his cowboy boots, which gave him an extra two or three inches. When Burt finally arrived and began sporting a different pair of cowboy boots each day, he was extremely pissed that the inserts were missing as each pair were specifically fitted for each pair of boots. Although he had his suspicions, he never found out that I was the one who had done the deed. A few days later I bribed one of the wardrobe girls to sneak into his room, while he was shooting, and lay all the lifts neatly on his bed. After that Burt's disposition improved with his extra inches.

I first met Angie Dickinson when I worked with her on a Movie of the Week entitled **Jealousy**. I always thought that she was a very beautiful lady from the first time I saw her in **Rio Bravo**. I was just a little kid when it aired on television and I still remember watching it with my father and having a crush on her.

I was her driver for the entire shoot and, of course, I was ecstatic about my good fortune. We became good friends and we both shared a mischievous sense of humor. One morning after I had picked her up for the day's shooting, she told me to pull the Town Car over to the curb right before we reached ABC Studios. I had no idea what was going through her mind and I was worried because we were running late as a result of a traffic jam on Coldwater Canyon.

Always totally playful, Angie had decided that she was going to drive me onto the set just to see everyone's reaction when we stepped out of the car. I exited the car and she slid over to the driver's side and I entered and sat in the passenger seat. She drove me up to the set and parked directly in front of the assembled cast and crew, insisting that she must open the door for me. When I got out of the car, everyone was either laughing or applauding. I instinctively took a little bow and we were soon at work. A great way to begin the day. Angie and I have always stayed in touch. She is a consummate lady that has retained a down-to-earth quality that makes you love her instantly.

Down and Out in Beverly Hills came next. Paul Mazurski directed the picture and I served as his driver. I met all the stars of the film, Richard Dryfus, Bette Midler, Tracy Nelson and, most interestingly, Nick Nolte. Nick Nolte was a piece of work. Before we began shooting, Paul had me pick him up at his home in Malibu. It was a Friday afternoon and Nick wanted me to drive him to skid row in downtown Los Angeles, where he had decided to live for the next four days to get acquainted with the plight of the homeless in order to enhance the vagrant he was playing in the movie. During that period of time he interacted with the homeless masses that reside there without showering or changing his clothes. I reconnected with him at our designated place on Monday afternoon and drove him back to Malibu. I don't think there is a greater contrast in the United States between two locations. At my request, we kept the windows of the van rolled down on the drive home.

The next week, as we shot his homeless sequences first, Nick was totally in character as the man who sneaks into Richard and Bette's Beverly Hills home. I don't know this for a fact, but rumor had it that he didn't shower for the entire week. When the shooting was wrapped, I was the one responsible for disposing of his clothes and it certainly seemed that way. I held my nose the best I could and put them in a garbage bag, dropping them in the nearest trash gondola. Whenever I watch **Down and Out in Beverly Hills** I always remember the smell of those well-worn clothes. Although I don't watch the film very often, I have to admit that his characterization of the homeless man was one of his best roles.

The Beverly Hills house had been constructed next to an existing swimming pool at the Warner Bros. Ranch, just north of the lot along Hollywood Way. This is where Nick attempts suicide at the beginning of the film and is one of the most memorable scenes. One day at lunchtime, Nick was observed urinating in the swimming pool so filming had to be wrapped that day. The next day the pool had to be drained, sanitized, and fresh water pumped into it.

Richard and Bette kept very much to themselves and occasionally I would talk to Tracy Nelson (Rick Nelson's daughter), who played their daughter. At the time she was looking forward to a film career, but unfortunately that never happened to the extent she had hoped.

During the shooting, if we wrapped early, I would occasionally go to the Whitsett Golf Course, a par three course and driving range just south of Ventura Boulevard in Studio City. When you have lived in the Los Angeles area as long as I have, you learn very quickly that you can run into a celebrity just about anywhere at any time. One time I decided to work on my long game so I went to the driving range where I met Max Baer, Jr., one of the stars of the mid-1960's hit show **The Beverly Hillbillies.** We chatted briefly and then hit some balls. Max hit the longest, straightest drives I have ever seen. Another time I was just going to play a round of golf by myself when Marty Feldman and his mother asked if they could join me. Playing golf with the two of them was fun and frustrating at the same time. They kibitzed and clowned around the whole time. I shot one of my worst games of golf EVER that day.

Working next on the television series **In the Heat of the Night** starring Carroll O'Connor and Howard Rollings was literally a "trip." Carroll was always very friendly and the consummate professional. Although he would sometimes joke around with the cast and crew, he kept to himself most of the time, staying in character.

Howard Rollings was a different story entirely. Rollings, as everyone knows, had a serious drug problem at the time, which resulted in his being banned from entering Louisiana for filming. He had been busted so many times that the paparazzi loved to dwell on his addiction. For this reason the powers that be in Louisiana told the producers of the show that he could not enter the state. Consequently, all the exterior shots that were supposed to be Mobile, Alabama's ocean front docks and beaches were actually shot in Long Beach.

During my short stay as transportation coordinator, I assigned a driver to Rollings whose duty was to watch him from the time he picked him up until we wrapped at the end of the day. I'm proud to say that during my tenure there were no problems or incidents with Rollings. Unfortunately, Carroll's son Hugh also had a drug problem. When he joined the series, I had him monitored on a daily basis as well and there were never any incidents. Sadly both Howard and Hugh eventually overdosed as a result of their drug use. I felt very bad because both men were always very friendly and in their own way charismatic.

Moving Violations with Bill Murray's brother John was my next assignment. While filming I had to teach Clara Pellar of Burger King's "Where's the beef?" fame how to drive. That was a real experience. One time she mistook the gas pedal for the brake and we flew into a garment rack that wardrobe had just wheeled over for some of the backgrounds players to hand their extra clothes. Luckily she didn't run over any cast, crew or background actors during her lesson. Other than that minor accident, she learned rather quickly and did a good job as a driver.

Once in awhile I'd have a day off and would go down to Hollywood Park. Like my father I loved horse racing and making small wagers on the horses. One day I happened to sit next to Mel Brooks, who had an affinity for the horses as well. He had quite an ego and loved talking about himself. When I managed to get a word or two into the "conversation," I asked him about working with Gene Wilder on **Blazing Saddles**. He said, "You know, everybody always asks me about that picture. Working with Gene was always a delight, but during the filming he was more quiet than usual on the set. I found out later that he was scribbling down notes on the future **Young Frankenstein**, which we would soon co-author." After awhile I could tell that he was tired of my company and questions about his films. He got up to make some bets and when he returned he sat about fifty feet away from me.

6

I began 1985 with an interesting assignment at NBC. Stephen J. Cannell was one of the busiest writer/producers in the industry. My job was to take care of Nick Mancuso on Cannell's television series **Stingray**. Stephen noticed the rapport that Nick and I had from the beginning and sensed that I was the only guy on the set who had the ability to keep Nick from misbehaving. Nick and I became good friends until they decided to film the show in Canada and we ended up losing contact with one another. Like most people you work with in the business, you lose contact very quickly when a production wraps or moves out of town. One day on the set a grip dropped something in the middle of Nick's scene. He angrily jumped out of character and told the entire cast, crew, and background players that he hated them all. Adding that he didn't want to work with any of them anymore. Stephen gave me a nod and I took him aside and explained that we all had to work together and it was best if he controlled his outbursts. After that he was fine, joking with people and even interacting with some of the background players. Perhaps I should have been a diplomat.

I also worked with Michael Landon on **Highway to Heaven** at MGM that year. Michael was one of the nicest guys that I ever worked with. He was especially respectful and gracious to all of the crew, which is not always the case with some actors, directors and producers. He would, for instance, give television sets to the entire crew at Christmas time and on Mondays he insisted that we always wrapped by 5 PM so everyone could go home and watch ABC's **Monday Night Football.** I once went to his house in Benedict Canyon, where I picked up him and his family and drove them to LAX. Almost all of us did little favors like that for him because he was always so friendly and generous. I mourn his passing at such a young age.

When 1986 rolled around, I couldn't believe that I had been working steadily for the past ten years. That year I worked on **Made in Heaven**, which was shot in South Carolina. Timothy Hutton, Debra Winger and the very beautiful Kelly McGillis were the stars, but when I recall that shoot I always think of Neil Young. Young, who was a friend of Alan Rudolph, the director, showed up on location one day for a cameo appearance in the film. I happened to have my little backpacker guitar with me and during a break from the shooting we sat on a curb a little distance away so as not to be disturbed and played guitar together for about a half and hour. Quite an experience jamming with Neil Young.

Another great guy to work with was Telly Savalas, where I served as his exclusive driver for the television movie **Hollywood Detective.** I would pick him up every morning at the Sheraton-Universal. He had a penthouse there and lived with his mother. He never called me Tony. He always called me Antwan. One day we had to drive to our location in Red Rock Canyon, which is up the 14 Freeway. As we were nearing the Mojave Desert, Telly had to take a piss. At the time no one knew it, but he had the first stage of prostate cancer. He said to me, "Hey, Antwan, I have to take a piss really bad."

"Okay," I said, "No problem we'll look for a restroom."

"No way," he urgently responded. "I gotta go now."

I pulled over and Telly took the longest piss along the 14 Freeway as a few cars and trucks zoomed by. I think it had to be the longest piss on record. We were already late for our call so once he got himself secured in the limo I started doing about 90 miles per hour along the relatively deserted freeway. Suddenly I noticed in the review mirror that a California Highway Patrolman was in pursuit on his motorcycle. His lights started flashing and I pulled to the side of the freeway.

Telly rolled down his window and said, Excuse me, officer, I'm late for work."

You should have seen the look on the officer's face when he realized that he was talking to Telly Savalas. The officer must have been a **Kojack** fan because he just waved us on our way without writing a ticket.

Alan King was also one of the nicest guys in the business. He was one of the best. I briefly drove him for the television series **Thirty Something** when Alan was making a guest star appearance. For some reason he really liked me and on the last day of shooting he asked me if I would drive him to LAX. We finished shooting in the morning and since he had a late afternoon flight he took me to the Palm on Santa Monica Boulevard for lunch, a very pricy restaurant, as a "thank you" for driving him to the airport.

a picture of Tony + Jeff

11 22'93

To Tony
Best Wishes
Telly Savalas

7

The first time I met Jeff Bridges was on the set of **The Fabulous Baker Boys**. It was 1988 and Jeff had established himself as a fine actor, who could bring big box office returns. The first thing I noticed was that both Jeff and his brother Beau were both much like Michael Landon...very generous and friendly to their fellow actors and the crew. I also discovered that Jeff liked his vodka and Beau liked his chardonnay after a long day's work.

One night the three of us found ourselves in one of the ballrooms at the Biltmore Hotel, where many of the interiors were being filmed. It was four in the morning and we had come to watch Michelle Pfeiffer slink around on a grand piano, while she sang 'Makin' Whoopee.' It seemed like the director, Steve Kloves, did an endless amount of takes and we loved every one.

Fortunately, I drove for Jeff for the entire picture. Little did I know, but my meeting Jeff would be to paraphrase Humphrey Bogart to Claude Raines in **Casablanca** "the beginning of a beautiful friendship."

Soon after **The Fabulous Baker Boys** I began work on **Hart to Hart Returns** with Robert Wagner and Stephanie Powers. It was one of several NBC **Friday Night Mystery Movies**, which also included **Columbo, Quincy**, and **Berretta**. As most people know Robert Wagner had everyone call him RJ and he was always a pleasure to work with. In the tradition of some of the Hollywood stars that he admired in his youth (Gary Cooper, Clark Gable, James Stewart and Fred Astaire) he was the perfect gentleman. Stephanie was also a pleasure to work with, but I got to know RJ much better than Stephanie.

Once he felt comfortable with me as a friend and he had confidence in me as a professional, he asked me to find the motor home that he had used in the original **Hart to Hart** series. When the series was produced in the 1980's the stars used mobile homes instead of the popular Star Wagons, used now and he wanted to use it on **Hart to Hart Returns.** I made a few calls and found it in a matter of about two days.

Not far from the NBC-Universal lot, the mobile home was located in Van Nuys at a storage yard near the Van Nuys Airport. When I informed RJ that I had located the mobile home he was ecstatic and had me drive to the storage yard immediately. With the description in mind and with the help of the yard manager, I found it very quickly. The manager had to take care of some other business and just handed me the keys and said, "Have a look."

Entering RJ's mobile home was like walking into a time warp. There were a variety of photographs on the walls in the bedroom and the living area of him and Natalie Wood. On the kitchenette counter sat several half-full bottles of liquor and a box of unopened crackers. The bed was unmade and there was a pair of pants and a shirt lying on the comforter. A pair of Topsiders sat on the floor next to a watermarked glass, where over the years the liquid that had been in it evaporated. The closet was filled with clothes and some racquetball equipment. The pictures of Natalie gave the whole place a kind of tomb-like quality like entering King Tut's chamber for the first time. I sat on the couch in the living area and looked at all the pictures of RJ and Natalie...they looked so young and happy just like all of us long ago. None of us knowing what the future would hold. Like most guys I had always been "in love" with Natalie and the whole vibe made me sadly nostalgic.

After a few minutes I broke from my reverie and called RJ to ask him what he wanted me to do with the mobile home's contents. I was shocked when he said, "Do whatever you want with it. I don't want any of it. If you want anything, take it." The first thing that crossed my mind was to remind him that some of Natalie's stuff was in there, but I left well enough alone. I couldn't bear to throw the pictures away so I went to the local Home Depot and purchased a few boxes. After cleaning out the cupboard, I threw away their contents as well as all the liquor bottles. I boxed up the clothes, racquetball equipment, and pictures, which consisted of three book boxes, and put them in a storage area in the bedroom. I kept Natalie's racquetball racquet, which I still have. When I left the site, I arranged for the manager to have the mobile home sent to the NBC-Universal lot, where RJ used it for the entire series.

On **Hart to Hart Returns** I made the mistake of hiring a non-union driver for Stephanie. NBC was always very budget conscious and they wanted to save some money. One day we were shooting on Castaic near the prison, which is west of Los Angles in the middle of nowhere. The driver missed her exit so she had to travel thirty miles round trip out of her way in order to return to Castaic.

Giving her a second chance, I gave her another task a little later in the week when we were shooting at Big Bear, a small mountain community north of Los Angeles. I sent her into town to have her make copies of the next day's call sheets. When she didn't return one of the locals came to the set. He informed me that one of the vans from our shoot was off the road and lying on its side. I immediately drove to the site with the local and sure enough there was the van. The driver was being extricated from the vehicle, having survived with a broken neck. The next day I had a union driver for Stephanie.

After a season on **Hart to Hart Returns** I was sent to Miami, assigned to pull and maintain Arnold Schwarzenegger's trailer on **True Lies**. Upon first meeting Arnold I was struck by his off-screen persona. He was nice enough, but very impersonal and very much the business man. He seemed less interested in making movies and more interested in making money. While filming **True Lies** he visited Cuba, where he was investigating the potential purchase of a cigar factory/plantation. Equally, while we were shooting the picture, he had several meetings with video game producers and companies. Arnold had the foresight to realize the future market for video games and the profits that could be made.

My duties as the caretaker of Arnold's trailer were relatively simple. I had to tow it to each location, keep it clean, and, most importantly, keep it stocked with cigars and Pilsner Urquell beer. One of the first things Arnold said to me in his iconic Austrian accent was, "Tony, I want to see no footprints on the carpet when I walk in every morning. Absolutely no footprints on the carpet." That simple task, achieved by backing my way out of the trailer as I vacuumed, kept us on great terms throughout the shoot.

One of our locations was Marathon, in the Florida Keys, where the famous bridge sequence was filmed. Although Florida is much more humid than southern California, the cast and crew got used to the change in a few days. Any discomfort was of little consequence because everyone had fun working with Arnold and his co-star, Jamie Leigh-Curtis.

The filming ended in Florida shortly after a break for the Christmas Holiday. I, along with some other crew members, were responsible for dismantling the base camp in Sugar Loaf Key and packing all the equipment and wardrobe for shipment back to Los Angeles. My job, after all the packing was completed, was to drive back to L. A. with Arnold's trailer in tow. All went well until I hit Fort Stockton, Texas. I stopped to fuel the cab and after topping it off I made a right turn out of the gas station. As I pulled out of the station the transmission fell apart. Fortunately, there was a Ford dealership nearby. I walked over and arranged to have the cab towed back to their lot for repairs. I explained to the dealership manager who I was and that the trailer belonged to Arnold

Schwarzenegger. A big fan of Arnold's he assured me that I would be on the road the next day. Knowing the cab would be repaired, I got a room at the motel near the dealership. The owner of the motel allowed me to park the trailer in his parking lot so I bought a six pack and I thought I would have a nice, relaxing evening in Fort Stockton, Texas. To my surprise a few hours later all these cars converged on the motel to look at Arnold's trailer. The manager of the hotel had told a few people that the trailer belonged to Arnold and word had spread fast. Soon the whole town appeared to see this small piece of Hollywood sitting in their town.

I left my room deciding that I would give Arnold's fans a real treat. The trailer had a back door and a side door so I told the people that they could come in for a tour. I brought them in through the back door and showed them Arnold's family pictures on the walls and one of the costumes he had worn in **True Lies**, which he hadn't returned to wardrobe. As the viewers exited through the side door, I gave them a cigar and a Planet Hollywood T-shirt since Arnold was promoting the Planet Hollywood restaurants at the time. When I telephoned Arnold and told him what I had done, he was very pleased. He said, "Good boy, Tony. You promote the picture and the restaurant. Good thinking, Tony. You're thinking like a businessman." The viewing of the trailer was featured in the local Fort Stockton newspaper the next day.

Returning to Los Angeles was a breeze and we began shooting in Van Nuys. The day the Northridge Earthquake hit. Obviously, no one made it to work that day, even though James Cameron, the director, expected the cast and crew to return for shooting that afternoon. Everyone was uneasy because there were still after-shocks throughout the Valley, but no one missed the call. We loved James, but he was a nose to the grindstone kind of director. No way would he allow an earthquake to interfere with his picture.

9

In 1995 I worked on **Broken Arrow** and got to know Christian Slater and Howie Long. Howie was a great guy and to my surprise showed an interest in the history of film. One day we went into the Photography Department at Twentieth-Century-Fox and dug up old stills of some of the famous stars of the Silver Screen---Tyrone Power, Rita Hayworth, Victor Mature, James Stewart and Susan Hayward. We had a blast just looking at them and talking about some of our favorite movies. Howie was very knowledgeable about film and many of its stars from that period, which was not something I expected from a football star. One of his favorite old movies was **My Darling Clementine**, which revolved around the famous gunfight at the OK Corral.

I got along well with Christian Slater too. He was just learning how to play the guitar so I often showed him a few licks in between shooting. He was a fast learner and by the time we got to Montana for the exteriors, Christian, me and some other guys on the crew played songs on many nights after we wrapped. There was nothing else to do. One night we even performed for the entire cast and crew. Luckily, by the time we played our audience had had enough adult beverages that they didn't notice the mistakes we made.

The producers on **Broken Arrow** were very generous. Later, when we were shooting at the southern rim of the Grand Canyon, they had the caterer prepare a prime rib and lobster lunch for the entire cast and crew. Since the Navajo Nation Reservation was located next to our location, we shared our lunch with the Navajos who were selling beads, blankets, jewelry and crafts that day. The lunch could have been a scene from a John Ford movie if it had been captured on film.

Working with Kyra Sedgwick and Forest Whitaker on **Phenomenon** was also a pleasure. Kyra is a lovely lady and we became friends, remaining in contact with one another to this day. At the film's premiere I was flattered when Kyra and her husband, Kevin Bacon, asked me to sit with them. Forest is not only a great actor but also a hell of a good guy. To say the least he is a party animal and a lady's man. Unbeknownst to him, at that time, he tried to pick up a girl I was dating. We still run into one another and to this day he still apologizes for hitting on her.

I followed **Phenomenon** with the feature **Michael**, shot in Texas and Chicago. Nora Ephron, the director, is one of the sweetest people and kindest directors I have ever known. Andie MacDowell and William Hurt were two of the stars, but they stayed pretty much to themselves throughout the shoot. Robert Pastorelli, who regrettably died later of a drug overdose, was very friendly and the only cast member who did any socializing with the crew.

After **Michael** I arranged for trailers and flatbeds to be transported from Chicago to Baltimore to be shipped to Paris, France via Brussels. The plan was to work with Roman Polanski, who was banned from filming in the United States, on his next picture entitled **The Double**. Although an incredible amount of money was spent on shipping and travel, the project was shutdown. I did, however, have a chance to meet John Goodman who was cast in the film. John and I had a couple of fun evenings in Paris. I also had lunch with Roman Polanski. I thought that he would probably express his disappointment for the demise of the film, but it didn't seem to concern him. Instead, he told me how he had escaped from Poland prior to World War II. Our conversation heightened when I told him about my Lithuanian ancestors, who had also escaped from their homeland during that period as well.

After spending six weeks in Paris, I drove to Brussels and arranged for all the equipment to be shipped back to Baltimore. Flying home I kept wishing that the film would have been made. I knew I would have had more fun in Paris and was sure I would have had more conversations with Roman. Arriving in Baltimore, I waited for the equipment. Without much to do, I attended an Oriels game, but I remember most watching the Fourth of July fireworks in Washington, D. C., which was just a short walk from my hotel. The equipment arrived rather quickly and I began my cross-country drive to Los Angeles.

Shortly after my return, I worked with director John Wu on **Faceoff** and got to know one of the film's stars, Nicolas Cage. We became close enough friends that several weeks later, he asked me to go to the docks in San Pedro to retrieve a vintage Ford GT that he had purchased from a sheik for a million dollars. Driving to the set from San Pedro in the GT, I felt like a million dollars myself on the 405 Freeway, taking the longest route possible before delivery. Driving up to the set in his new toy, Nick was like a little kid on Christmas Day with a new bicycle. He jumped in the car and took it for a short drive before shooting resumed.

Nick also had a workout trailer and he and I, along with a couple of other drivers, would workout everyday and shoot the shit like we were back in high school. Nick and I never socialized past the workday, but he was always very friendly and never seemed like he thought of himself as a "star."

The General's Daughter was my next picture and my personal favorite because I met my girlfriend, Kim Ruha, on Stage Five of Paramount Studios. At the time Kim was working for the American Humane Association. In a scene where a cat was to walk through a pool of blood from a bleeding James Woods, Kim was on the set to make sure that the cat was treated properly. From that day to this (eighteen years later) Kim and I are still in love, but not married...we, like Kurt and Goldie, don't want to screw-up the relationship with a marriage license.

James Woods was one crazy guy to work with. He is as great an actor as he is "crazy." He loved to stir things up with director Simon West and the cast and crew. He very often set in motion some trivial incident that got everyone shook-up. The most memorable was the time he spread the rumor that someone had tampered with the salad during our lunch break. After lunch the caterer couldn't understand why his beautiful salad had been untouched.

I also worked as a stand-in and double for James Cromwell on the picture. While filming on location in Savannah, Georgia, Simon had me do eight takes where I had to run over three blocks on this uneven terrain. I cursed him when I could hardly walk the next day. Simon's signature saying, after almost every take, was "One more for luck." On the last day of shooting we were in Sacramento on a bridge. The cast and crew were totally worn out after an endless amount of takes from a number of different angles. When Simon said, "One more for luck," the entire crew walked out and left him standing on the bridge alone to which he said, "I guess that's a wrap."

Primary Colors, directed by Mike Nichols, was a film about Bill Clinton and his escapades before and during his time in the White House. Billy Bob Thorton and Kathy Bates were the highlight of that shoot. Billy Bob and I have remained friends and like Forest Whitaker the two of us bump into one another around Los Angeles or on an occasional project. Working with him was like working with an old friend...some drinking, partying and just fooling around on the set. I just recently work with him on **Bad Santa 2** and it was just like old times. Kathy very often joined in our rowdiness, but most of all I loved watching her perform. She was always the total actress and then suddenly herself when we wrapped for the day.

10

Working on **What Women Want** with Mel Gibson and Helen Hunt was more memorable for Mel than for me. Mel and I became fast friends when I told him that I had had lunch with Moe Howard of The Three Stooges. Mel loved the Stooges and was delighted when I gave him a moment to moment retelling of the story. His favorite part of the story was, of course, that I had told Moe that Curly was my favorite Stooge.

Town and Country was directed by Peter Chelsom and starred Warren Beatty and Diane Keaton. At a cost of $90 million it grossed only $3.5 million. To say the least, it was an absolute disaster. Beatty was so difficult to work with that Chelsom walked off the set one day and let him direct the day's shoot. Beatty took it in his stride and enjoyed his new "role" for the day. After the film's debacle, Warner Bros. would not involve itself with another Warren Beatty picture until **Rules Don't Apply** in which he not only starred but also served as director.

The picture took almost a year and a half to make and I was doing some driving on the last days of the re-shoots. Because it was Diane Keaton's last day, she had booked an evening flight from Los Angles to New York, where she was contractually bound to begin a new project.

Warren decided that he didn't want to do anymore shooting for the day, which meant that Diane would have to cancel her flight to New York. As I leaned against the property trailer drinking a ginger ale, Diane, who had talked to me earlier about my driving her on **Looking for Mr. Goodbar**, stormed by nodding and saying, 'Hi, Tony,' heading for his trailer without missing a step.

She halted at the door and began knocking. When Warren didn't answer she yelled, "You come out of there you son-of-a-bitch and shoot me out *today* or you lose me for good."

He came out of his trailer smiling and in his charming manner said, "Of course, Diane. We're gonna shoot you out today. I was just taking a nap."

Diane replied, "You bet your ass you're gonna shoot me out."

She turned and stormed back to her trailer. During the course of the afternoon Diane finished her scenes and I drove her to LAX for her scheduled flight.

Goldie Hawn also worked on the picture. During some location shooting in South Pasadena, I introduced myself and told her how Kurt Russell and I had bonded years earlier when we worked on **Elvis.** Goldie was very busy that day, but she took some time to chat with me, knowing that if Kurt liked me I had to be a decent person to talk with.

Charlton Heston made a cameo appearance early on in the film. At this point in his career he was up in years and in failing health. For one of the pick-up shots Chelsom needed the bathrobe he had worn on the original shoot. Heston had kept the robe and it was at his house in Beverly Hills. My assignment that afternoon was to retrieve the robe. Heston's housekeeper had been notified that I would be arriving so after entering the house he escorted me up stairs to Heston's bedroom. The housekeeper opened the closet door, revealing a soiled, stained, smelly robe hanging proudly next to many other garments almost in the same condition. I told the housekeeper that I wasn't going to touch the robe. It was that bad. He understood and placed it in a garbage bag for its journey back to the set. After arriving on the set, I took it directly to wardrobe, where they miraculously cleaned it for the shot.

Following my work on **Town and Country** I got a call from a friend who was working on a low-budget, non-union film entitled **Tea with Grandma.** He asked me if I could drive out to Tippi Hedron's ranch/compound known as the Shambala Animal Preserve in Acton, north of Los Angeles. There Tippi had all kinds of rescued animals, including tigers, lions, and other exotic and domestic beasts. As a favor he wanted me to pick her up for the day's shooting in Commerce on Sunday.

My girlfriend Kim, who was still associated with the Humane Association, and I left my home in Calabasas early and drove to Shambala. We were both looking forward to meeting Tippi and having a look at all the animals. As we drove up her remote driveway, we exchanged apprehensive looks as we were greeted by the sound of roaring lions. We wondered what we had gotten ourselves into. After parking the car and walking to her door, we had to knock several times. Finally she answered the door, looking a bit disheveled and said she would be out in a few minutes. We were surprised that she didn't ask us in, but we didn't give it another thought as we wanted to have a look around the compound and see some of her animals. There were two very tame lions, one tiger that growled at us, a few zebras, a giraffe, some goats, sheep and on and on. It was truly a managerie and we were amazed that she took care of all the animals with just one caretaker to help. The lions were the most memorable. They came right next to us and rubbed their faces on the fence as if they expected us to pet them just like a house cat.

About a half hour later, Tippi came out of the house and she talked with us about all the animals that she had saved. None of which were birds. No surprise there. I'm convinced that if we would have had time she could have told us the history of every animal in Shambala, but we were on a tight schedule so we drove off.

Approaching Los Angeles, she asked if we could stop at her daughter Melanie Griffth's house in Hancock Park, where she was living with Antonio Bandaras. Tippie needed to pick up some jewelry. We parked in Melanie's driveway and Melanie, who knew she was stopping by, came out and they greeted one another with a hug. Tippi and Melanie entered the house and once again Kim and I sat in the car for another half hour. Finally, Tippi exited the house and we were off to Commerce. During the drive, she reminisced about Alfred Hitchcock's extended crush on her, while filming both **The Birds**. How she had to very often escape his advances during filming in Santa Cruz by driving around the countryside in the Aston Marten used in the film. She also mentioned how she, like all the other actors in the picture, were abused by so many birds that it interfered with the comity between the actors and Hitchcock in particular. Unfortunately the drive was over all too soon and she didn't have time to give us anymore details. She basically said that the whole experience filming **The Birds** was a nightmare and that she had never been happier to wrap a shoot.

Working with Jim Carey on **The Majestic** was fun. The last evening of shooting, however, is the most memorable. My friend Craig Lieteke and I were standing on a cliff in Griffth Park, looking out at the Los Angeles city lights. During the entire shoot Jim had arranged for the In-N-Out burger truck to be on location at least three times a week for our second meal at his expense. Jim loved the burgers. While Craig and I were chatting, Jim walked up behind us. He joined our conversation and we all agreed how much fun the entire shoot had been and we were grateful for his generosity supplying the In-N-Out truck. He smiled in the typical Jim Carrey leer and said, "Boys, you know why I did it? Because I'm filthy rich." He had just received a $70 million bonus for **The Grinch.**

After **The Majestic** I worked on John Frankenheimer's last film **A Path to War**, which was about LBJ's decision not to run for re-election to the Presidency of the United States in 1968, based on the toll the war in Vietnam had taken on him. During the shooting I drove Michael Gambon, who had arrived in Los Angeles after a successful television series in the United Kingdom entitled **The Singing Detective**. Today Gambon is best known for his role as Dumbledore in the **Harry Potter** films.

I also met Alec Baldwin and Donald Sutherland on the picture. One afternoon we were all standing around the catering tent. Alec somehow knew that I had worked with Jeff Bridges on **The Fabulous Baker Boys** and that I was planning to go to New York to work on a movie with Jeff and Kim Bassinger based on John Irving's story 'Door in the Floor.' Alec was going through a heated divorce with Kim at the time and he asked me, "Could we talk privately for a few minutes?"

I said, "Sure."

Going to an isolated area behind the tent, he said, "I know you're working on **Door in the Floor**. Here's my cell number. I want you to keep me posted on what Kim does everyday."

I instinctively backed away and said, "I can't do that. What Kim does is none of my business and I never do that sort of thing."

He was cool about it and said, "Alright, that's fine. I totally understand."

After that encounter I sensed that he must have been a very controlling man.

Talking with Donald Sutherland was much more fun. I asked him about a memorable scene in **Space Cowboys** with his co-stars Clint Eastwood, James Garner and Tommy Lee Jones. I was particularly interested in the scene where he rides the roller coaster, eating a banana and asked, "How many bananas did you have to eat for that scene?"

He said, "Tony, we did four takes. I hate rollercoasters and bananas so after every take, I threw-up."

11

I worked on **The O. C.** for a couple of years, which was a very pleasurable experience. The hours were long and there was a lot of location shooting, adding an always welcome variety to the day's work. Peter Gallagher was fun to talk with and I became lasting friends with Kim Delaney, who along with numerous other actors and actresses guest starred on the show. I first met Eliot Cates at that time and helped him get some work on the series. Eliot worked so often that he told me later that he felt like a cast member.

My most memorable evening was driving Mischa Barton to her boyfriend Brandon Davis' house in Bel-Air. On the way to his house she changed in the back seat of the Town Car. By the time we arrived at his gate she had changed into a sexy chiffon dress minus a bra. I pressed the button on the gate, but there was no response. Mischa was unset and hurriedly asked, "Tony, what are we going to do?" I said, "Don't worry, I know what to do." I exited the car and forced the gate open far enough for her to squeeze her very slim body through without soiling her dress. Once she was inside the gate she asked me if I would drive her and Brandon to the Sunset Strip for a night of partying. I politely refused, explaining that it was not my job and knowing if I would have driven her I would have spent an all-nighter in the car, waiting outside the Viper Club or some other popular place at the time.

Shortly after **The O. C.** I found myself reunited with Jeff Bridges, who was starring in **Seabiscuit**. I had enjoyed working with Jeff on **The Fabulous Baker Boys** and was pleased to be working on another picture with him. In this business many of the people you work with you never see again and in some cases that's a good thing. But Jeff and I had had a bit of bonding on our first picture and I think he was excited to see me and have me drive for him. As his driver/assistant I drove him all over southern California and booked his stay at countless hotels during the filming. His favorite hotel was the Four Seasons in Beverly Hills. When we were shooting in Los Angeles, Jeff always stayed there. I would, of course, drive him to the Four Seasons every day when we wrapped, but instead of going to his room he liked to sit in the Town Car outside the entrance. Jeff and I chatted while we smoked a couple of cigars and drank a few "tall" vodkas...his favorites were Grey Goose, Tito and Skyy. Listening to the radio and talking, he loved to pay attention to who arrived and exited the hotel.

If Jeff saw someone he knew, it was my job to get out of the Town Car, introduce myself, and cajole him or her to join us for a chat and a drink or both. The whole thing was like a precursor to one of today's reality shows. I still think it would be a great reality show...**Outside the Four Seasons with Jeff Bridges**, not unlike the drive and coffee show that Jerry Seinfeld does. Rosie Perez, Lionel Ritchie and Mischa Barton are only a few of the celebrities I remember chit-chatting with Jeff from the backseat of the car. One night the opposite happened. Shaquille O'Neal sent his driver over to us because he wanted to meet Jeff, who loved the role reversal. I told the driver to have Shaq come over.

When he arrived I got out of the car and shook hands with him before he got in the back seat. I said, "Great to meet you, but I have to confess. I'm a Pistons fan."

He looked at me with his trademark smile and said, "I'm sorry to hear that, but I understand."
One thing I loved about Jeff from the beginning: Although he has been very successful, he is one of the most humble stars I have ever known.

Jeff and I became such good friends on the **Seabiscuit** shoot that he insisted on my being contractually bound to drive for him in a series of movies. Our next picture was **Iron Man,** where Jeff played the villain Obadiah Stain, along with Iron Man, Robert Downey, Jr., and Pepper Potts, Gwyneth Paltrow. We shot the interiors at the Howard Hughes Hangar-Soundstage in Playa Vista. During the shooting, Gwyneth's knee went out and she had to be carried onto the set, which was raised almost a story off the floor. She was always so grateful and, like Jeff, very humble and totally fun on the set. Equally, Robert is very much like the two of them, very friendly and kind to everyone. My friend Eliot and his then girlfriend, Leslie, attended the **Iron Man** wrap party, where he and Leslie ended up talking to Robert for about a half hour. Eliot told me later that it was like talking to someone he had known forever. About four years later, Eliot ran into Robert at a Starbuck's in Malibu and told me that he remembered him from the party and they had another little chat over coffee.

Jeff next got a cameo role in **How to Lose Friends and Alienate People** with Simon Pegg and Kirsten Dunst. Although it was only a cameo appearance, we ended up staying in London for twenty-three days. That picture must have had a bottomless budget. Of the twenty-three days, Jeff only worked five. Today we both reflect on that stay in London as a lovely paid vacation. We not only partied quite a bid, but we also took in some of the sites. As an artist Jeff was particularly impressed with the Tate Gallery, which houses a variety of modern and post-modern pieces.

Never driven by the necessity of making huge amounts of money, Jeff next chose to do a series of low-budget films because he like the script and his co-stars. The first picture was **The Amateurs** (a.k.a. **The Moguls**) written and directed by Michael Traeger. Besides Jeff the film had an unbelievable cast, including Ted Danson, Tim Blake Nelson, Joe Pantoliano, William Fichtner, Patrick Fugit,

John Hawkes, Glenne Headly, Lauren Graham, Jeanne Tripplehorn, Isaih Washington, Steven Weber, Valerine Perrine, Judy Greer, Eileen Brennan, Brad Garrett and my good friend Eliot Cates. After doing countless commericials, Eliot was excited about being cast with so many stars. He and Ted, both of whom are straight as arrows, still delight in the fact that they were cast opposite one another as lovers.

Following the day's wrap, there was usually a party in Jeff's trailer. Very often it had the appearnce of a Gentleman's Club that occasionally allowed a few women. There was a lot of drinking and cigar smoking and story telling. Eliot, who was a devout fan of the ill-fated Michael Cimino film **Heaven's Gate,** loved talking with Jeff, who appeared in the movie, about the filming of the picture. Jeff had some great tales about the filming of the gunflight between the cattlemen and the immigrants, the climax of the film.

The Amateurs was one of those rare pictures where everyone totally enjoyed performing and partying. Eliot ran into Bill Fichtner at a dry cleaner in Toluca Lake one day and they reminisced for a few minutes. Bill told him, "That was the most fun I ever had on a picture."

Jeff followed **The Amateurs** with **Stick It**, written and directed by Jessica Bendinger, who had gained notoriety with the film **Bring It On**. In **Stick It** Jeff played the coach of a girls' gymnastics team. Without naming names there was a lot of promiscuity on that picture. Eliot, who worked briefly as Jeff's stand-in, and I both enjoyed that aspect of the shoot, along with the younger guys on the crew. Jeff as always was true-blue to his wife Susan.

Next we traveled to New York to film **A Dog Year** for HBO, based on the book by John Katz. In that picture Jeff played opposite a border collie. As the saying goes, 'Never share a scene with a child or an animal.' Jeff firmly believes to this day that the border collie stole the show. During the filming of **A Dog Year** we spent three weeks in Manhattan, three weeks in White Plains and Westchester, New York, then another three weeks in the farm country of Vermont. There I booked a group of bugalows about six miles from our location just across the border in upstate New York. With not much to do in the evening, Jeff, Susan and I sat up late at night. Jeff would play guitar and I would play harmonica to entertain whoever stopped by.

My last picture with Jeff was **Tron: Legacy** shot in Vancouver, Canada. The picture was mostly filmed on blue/green screen. What I remember most about that shoot was meeting the beautiful Olivia Wilde, a truly lovely lady. We stayed in Vancouver for three months and worked seven days a week. We barely had time for anything with the exception of a little exercise in Stanley Park.

After **Tron: Legacy** Jeff decided to take a lengthy hiatus. He was totally worn out from the strenuous shoot. I returned to the television series **The Mentalist**, which I had worked on periodically between Jeff's movies. While I stayed on **The Mentalist**, Jeff returned to film **Crazy Heart** for which he won an Academy Award for Best Actor.

Soon after **The Mentalist** folded, I drove Helen Merren for some pick-up shots for the film **Woman in Gold**. The two adjectives that come to mind when I think of Helen are "lovely" and "classy." Not only is she a great actress, but she also has absolutely no air of self-importance, and her energy is like that of someone half her age.

One morning I picked her up for an early call at her Tudor-style house at the foot of LaBrea in the Hollywood Hills. She was always very punctual, waiting for me to arrive and drive her to our location at the Hollywood Forever Cemetery. Thinking that she was running late, although it was only 5:45 AM, we pulled out of her driveway as I insisted that she wasn't late. Arriving at the light at Outpost Drive to make a left onto Franklin, she bcame impatient with the amount of time we were spending at the light. Suddenly she exited the Town Car, ran across the street, and punched the "walk" button, and then ran back and got into the car saying, "That ought to speed things up." The light turned green and off we went. We arrived at the Hollywood Forever Cemetery before most of the crew.

Another time we wrapped around 2:00PM. Before driving her home she wanted to do some shopping for clothes. I thought to myself "I'm getting off from work early for a change and now I have to drive her to Beverly Hills...probably Rodeo Drive...and deal with an afternoon of shopping.

I smiled and asked, "Beverly Hills, then?"

Helen said, "No, no, of course not. Let's just stop at the local Ross store."

I drove her to the Ross on Sunset and LaBrea and she went in, while I waited in the car. In less than a half hour she came out clutching two or three bags. I got out and helped her with the bags and in no time she was back home.

12

I'm currently working on the television series **Superstore** shot at Universal, right where I began forty-three years ago. The series stars America Ferrera, who played the title role in **Ugly Betty** a few years ago. Not only is working with America and the rest of the cast and crew fun, I still have the opportunity to meet some great actors, including veteran character actor Linda Porter who is a regular on the series in the role of Myrtle.

Just the other day I had the good fortune to drive Bernie Kopell, best known for his role as Dr. Adam Ricker on **The Love Boat**. He had guest starred on **Superstore** and I was assigned to drive him home when we wrapped. We had a delightful conversation from the lot to his home in Encino. In that short time period he told me about how he was a waiter, a bus driver, and a taxi driver until he got his start doing stand-up comedy. Early on in his career he had worked with Jack Benny, adding that he was one of the nicest stars he ever shared a stage with. At the other end of the spectrum was Milton Berle. He reminisced about appearing on **The Milton Berle Show** as a guest star with Martha Raye when he was very young. Throughout the rehearsal, Berle, who also directed the show, wore a whistle around his neck like a coach. Every time the actors didn't perform to his liking he would angrily blow the whistle. Unfortunately, we reached Bernie's house all too soon. I wished that we would have had a longer drive so I could hear more stories about the famous and infamous. I'm sure he had a million of them from **The Love Boat** alone.

Soon after my drive with Bernie, Eliot and I were driving to Paradise Cove to meet his former girlfriend Leslie for a few drinks and some dinner. I hadn't seen her in a long time and she said she was bringing a girl friend so I knew we'd have fun. Eliot was driving his Audi TT Roadster with the top down...the cloudless sky providing plenty of sunshine. It always feels good to have someone else drive. As we descended the grade on Kanan Road to Malibu, the expanse of the vast Pacific loomed before us, the Channel Islands in greens and greys silhouetted against the sky and ocean. Perhaps because he was thinking about his break-up with Leslie, Eliot waxed philosophical and said, "You know, Tony, I have been given a lot of gifts in my life and I squandered them all, pursuing a dream that I never quite realized. Women who love me and friends I threw away. When I leave this world I hope I can return and appreciate the gifts more."

I think he surprised himself when he said it. It was like he was almost thinking out loud. I know he surprised me. I said, "I think everyone our age thinks that."

He smiled and said, "Yeah, you're probably right."

I feel a little differently than Eliot. Just the other day I ran into Adam Arkin, who is the Executive Producer for the new television series **Get Shorty** with Ray Romano. We talked for awhile and we both started laughing when we remembered playing basketball with the guys from **Happy Days** a lifetime ago on the Paramount lot.

When we parted I looked nostalgically around the Universal lot, where I began, realizing, to use a cliché, that I had come full-circle and for the most part my career has brought many happy days. To most of the world I have left "no footprints on the carpet," but for me I have far exceeded my dreams and expectations so many years ago.

Kirsten Stoner is an animator and cartoonist based in Burbank, CA. She started making cartoons back in her junior year of high school and created her Little Animated Me characters. She then started the strip at the beginning of her freshman year of college and continued until the present day. With over 70 comic strips, she demonstrates sweet scenarios of everyday situations with either a comedic or sentimental ending. She focuses on putting a humorous spin on everyday life through humorous gags and relatable commentary. Currently, Kirsten is an animation student at Cal State Northridge. In addition to her comics, she is animating videos designed to aid people interested in animation as well as working as a freelance animator and illustrator.

Printed in the United States
By Bookmasters